Hamlet
Prince of Denmark

Right: The ghost of Hamlet's father appears on the battlements of Elsinore to demand, "Revenge his foul and most unnatural murder." (I, v) Hamlet makes his companions swear never to speak of what they have seen.

> **"**
>
> For this relief much thanks: 'tis bitter cold, And I am sick of heart *(I, i)*
>
> Neither a borrower nor a lender be; For loan oft loses both itself and friend ... This above all: to thine own self be true ... *(I, iii)*
>
> Something is rotten in the state of Denmark *(I, iv)*
>
> There are more things in heaven and earth, Horatio, Than are dreamt of in your philosophy *(I, v)*
>
> Though this be madness, yet there is method in't *(II, ii)*
>
> To be, or not to be: that is the question: Whether 'tis nobler in the mind to suffer The slings and arrows of outrageous fortune, Or to take arms against a sea of troubles, And by opposing end them? To die: to sleep: No more; and by a sleep to say we end The heartache and the thousand natural shocks That flesh is heir to, – 'tis a consummation Devoutly to be wish'd. To die, to sleep; To sleep: perchance to dream: ay, there's the rub: For in that sleep of death what dreams may come, When we have shuffled off this mortal coil, Must give us pause ... *(III, i)*
>
> I must be cruel, only to be kind ... *(III, iv)*
>
> The rest is silence *(V, ii)*
>
> **"**

King Hamlet of Denmark is dead, but his uneasy ghost paces the battlements of Elsinore, his former castle — his brother Claudius is now King and marries his widow, Queen Gertrude, with unseemly haste — Prince Hamlet, revolted at this 'incestuous' betrayal and devastated by his father's death, considers suicide even though he has been assiduously courting Ophelia, daughter of the court's Lord Chamberlain Polonius — Prince Hamlet, told by his dearest friend Horatio of the ghost, casts thoughts of suicide aside — he visits the battlements at midnight where the ghost tells him that Claudius murdered him by pouring poison in his ear, after seducing his wife Gertrude — he demands revenge — Prince Hamlet feigns madness and as part of his act scorns Ophelia's affections — a group of travelling tragedians call — Prince Hamlet asks them to perform for the court a classic play that closely duplicates King Hamlet's betrayal — Hamlet calculates that if Claudius is guilty he will give himself away — when the player King is murdered, flustered Claudius rises and the court leaves in disarray — Hamlet, convinced of Claudius' guilt, determines upon revenge — alarmed and suspicious, Claudius asks Polonius to engineer a meeting between Hamlet and his mother Gertrude and spy on them — Hamlet reacts so stormily to Gertrude that Polonius, hidden behind a tapestry, fears he may kill her and cries out — Hamlet, believing the spy to be Claudius, stabs him — Hamlet assures Gertrude he is not insane, hints at King Hamlet's murder and swears her to secrecy — Gertrude immediately betrays him to Claudius who sends Hamlet to England with Rosencrantz and Guildenstern, former friends of Hamlet's, purportedly for his own protection, but in reality with a letter asking the King of England to kill him — Laertes, Polonius' son, arrives with a mob to exact revenge — meanwhile Hamlet sends word that he is returning on a pirate ship that intercepted his own vessel — in reality he secretly opened the letter and substituted a forgery asking the King of England to kill Rosencrantz and Guildenstern, a request he complied with — Laertes, conspiring with Claudius, challenges Hamlet to a fencing match using a foil whose tip is laced with poison, with a celebratory cup of poisoned wine in reserve — Ophelia, Laertes' sister, driven insane by Hamlet's "madness" and her father's murder, drowns herself, further inflaming Laertes desire for revenge — The duel commences before the court — Hamlet initially wins some cuts — Gertrude drinks a toast to her son, but it is the poisoned chalice — Laertes wounds Hamlet, but in the scuffling that ensues Hamlet takes possession of the poisoned rapier and wounds Laertes — dying, Laertes tells Hamlet of the plot — Hamlet stabs Claudius and forces him too to drink the poisoned wine — only faithful Horatio, prevented from suicide by Hamlet, remains to tell the world the truth — King Hamlet originally won his lands from the King of Norway, and it is his son Fortinbras who now takes control — the Danish royal family is no more

DRAMATIS PERSONAE

Claudius . . . . King of Denmark
Hamlet . . . . son to the late,
 . . . . and nephew to the present, king
Gertrude . . . . Queen of Denmark, and
 . . . . mother to Hamlet
Fortinbras . . . . Prince of Norway
Horatio . . . . friend to Hamlet
Polonius . . . . Lord Chambelain
Laertes . . . . his son
Ophelia . . . . daughter to Polonius
Reynaldo . . . . servant to Polonius
Voltimand ⎫
Cornelius ⎪
Rosencrantz ⎬ courtiers
Guildenstern ⎪
Osric ⎪
A gentleman ⎭
A priest
Marcellus ⎫ officers
Bernardo ⎭
Francisco, a soldier
A captain
English ambassadors
Players
Grave-diggers

THEMES

● Revenge
● Madness
● Suicide
● Political corruption
● The relationship between real life and theatre

Above: Hamlet discovers the skull of the court's jester. "Alas, poor Yorick. I knew him, Horatio: a fellow of infinite jest, of most excellent fancy." (V, i)

Written between 1599 and 1601, Hamlet was first published in a quarto edition in 1603 and probably first performed in 1602. It is one of the most popular and frequently revived of Shakespeare's plays

Below: Claudius' panic reaction to the murder in the play exposes his guilt in his brother's murder.

Above: Ophelia and Hamlet. As part of his "madness" he cruelly pretends to renounce her love, but the result is to help drive her to madness herself and suicide by drowning. "Be thou as chaste as ice, as pure as snow, thou shalt not escape calumny. Get thee to a nunnery, go. Farewell." (III, i)

The Merry Wives of Windsor

> " Come, gentlemen, I hope we shall drink down all unkindness *(I, i)*
>
> If there be no love in the beginning, yet heaven may decrease it upon better acquaintance, when we are married and have more occasion to know one another: I hope, upon familiarity will grow more contempt *(I, i)*
>
> Why then the world's mine oyster, / Which I with sword will open *(II, ii)*
>
> This is the short and long of it *(II, ii)*
>
> Pinch him, fairies, mutually; / Pinch him for his villainy; / Pinch him, and burn him, and turn him about, / Till candles and starlight and moonshine be out. *(V, v)*
>
> I do begin to perceive that I am made an ass *(V, v)* "

Falstaff is in debt and decides to court two comfortably bourgeois Windsor ladies, Mistress Ford and Mistress Page, for fun and money — when his followers, Pistol and Nym, they refuse to deliver his love letters, he fires them — in revenge, they tell the husbands of the fat knight's intrigues — Page is phlegmatic, but jealous Ford disguises himself as "Brook" to see if his wife is true — meanwhile Anne Page, Mistress Page's daughter, is besieged by suitors: Slender, Mr Page's protégé; Doctor Caius, Mistress Page's favoured suitor, and Fenton, whom Anne loves — Mistress Page is stunned to receive Falstaff's letter and flabbergasted when Mistress Ford arrives bearing an exact replica — together, they plot their response, helped by Mistress Quickly, Caius' servant — she is despatched to ask Falstaff to visit Mistress Ford when her husband will be out and tells him that Mistress Page has also fallen for his charms — meanwhile "Brooke" (Mr Ford) offers Falstaff money to seduce Mistress Ford so that it will be easier to make love to her himself — delighted, Falstaff reveals his clandestine assignation — alone, Brook is beside himself — meanwhile at the Ford household, Mistresses Ford and Page prepare for Falstaff's discomfiture, by telling the servants that the instant they call, the laundry basket must be taken out and dropped in a muddy ditch — Falstaff arrives for his appointment with Mistress Ford, but within moments Mistress Page arrives — Falstaff hides, only to hear Mistress Page deliver the news that Mr Ford is on his way home — in panic, Falstaff dives into the laundry basket, which is duly dumped in the ditch — too late, Mr Ford, searches in vain for Falstaff and finds he must apologise to the ladies — his jealous discomfort increases when later Falstaff tells him, as Brook, of his dunking and yet another assignation — Falstaff's plans are again foiled by the arrival of Mistress Page informing her friend that Mr Ford is on his way home — this time Falstaff is disguised in clothes belonging to Mistress Ford's maiden aunt — Mr Ford hates this woman and, seeing "her" there, beats her roundly and drives her from his house — Mistresses Ford and Page now decide to let their husbands in on the fun and pranks — Ford promises to give up his jealous ways, and together they plan a final mortification — Herne, an antler-headed god purportedly haunts an oak in a nearby forest, and it is in this guise that Falstaff is invited to meet Mistress Ford at midnight — he arrives full of passion and greets both the mistresses heartily, but in their wake appear many "fairies" and "satyrs" who are Anne and others dressed up — these creatures taunt and torment Falstaff mercilessly, terrifying him — Caius and Slender, Anne's suitors, are there and both erroneously lead boy "fairies" from the forest, thinking them to be Anne — who meanwhile has run off with Fenton — at last the wives confess their pranks, and Falstaff sees how he has been made a fool — Anne and her new husband are embraced by her family

DRAMATIS PERSONAE

Mistress Ford / Alice	
Frank Ford / Brook	her husband
Mistress Page / Margaret / Meg	
George Page	her husband
William Page	their son
Anne Page	their daughter
Fenton }	suitors for the hand of Anne Page
Slender }	
Caius	a doctor
Peter Simple	servant to Slender
John Rugby	servant to Caius
Mistress Quickly	servant to Caius
Falstaff	an improvident and rascally knight
Robin	his page
Bardolph, Pistol, Nym	
	members of Falstaff's company
Shallow	a justice of the peace
Sir Hugh Evans	a clergyman
Host	landlord of the Garter inn

Above: Falstaff arrives in good humour for his assignation with Mistress Ford. "'Have I caught my heavenly jewel?' Why, now let me die, for I have lived long enough: this is the period of my ambition. O this blessed hour!" MISTRESS FORD: " O sweet Sir John!" FALSTAFF: Mistress Ford, I cannot cog. I cannot prate, Mistress Ford. Now shall I sin in my wish ..." (III, iii)

Written probably about 1596–7, and performed in 1597, *The Merry Wives of Windsor* was first published in quarto in 1602. Mainly in prose, this boisterous farce concerns middle-class marital infidelity, its central player being Falstaff, the fat knight from *Henry IV* and *Henry V* – tradition has it that the play was inspired by a request from Queen Elizabeth for a comedy featuring this popular character.

Left: Sir John hides in the laundry basket, unaware of Mistress Ford's instructions to her servants, "and when I suddenly call you come forth, and without any pause or staggering, take this basket on your shoulders: that done, trudge with it in alll haste, and carry it among the whitsters in Datchet-mead, and there empty it in the muddy ditch close by the Thames side." (III, iii)

Above: Fenton and Anne Page steal away to be married. But her parents are happy – MISTRESS PAGE: Master Fenton, Heaven give you many, many merry days! Good husband, let us every one go home, And laugh this sport o'er by a country fire; Sir John and all." (V, v)

As You Like It

Above: Orlando's love-letters are discovered by Rosalind (in the guise of Ganymede) pinned to the trees of the forest. ORLANDO: " O Rosalind! these trees shall be my books, And in their barks my thoughts I'll character ..." (III, ii)

> All the world's a stage / And all the men and women merely players. / They have their exits and their entrances; / And one man in his time plays many parts ... (II, vii)
>
> Blow, blow, thou winter wind! / Thou art not so unkind / As man's ingratitude (II, vii)
>
> Can one desire too much of a good thing? (IV, i)

Duke Frederick has usurped his brother Duke Senior, who with a band of followers is now in exile in the Forest of Arden — Oliver, who as elder son of the deceased Sir Roland de Boys, has inherited his entire fortune, hates his younger brother Orlando, who plans to make his fortune through wrestling — he begins by challenging, in disguise, the vicious prize fighter Charles — Celia and Rosalind attend the match — Orlando triumphs, and he and Rosalind fall in love — Frederick, suspecting Rosalind of treachery, banishes her — disguised as "Ganymede", a young man, she makes her way to the forest of Arden with Celia, who is disguised as Ganymede's sister "Aliena" — Orlando, and Oliver's father has been an enemy of Frederick's — and when the Duke hears that Rosalind and Celia were admiring Orlando and may have left with him, he is furious — he calls for Oliver and tells him to deal with Orlando or risk losing his fortune — a faithful servant warns Orlando not to return home, as Oliver plans to burn him alive as he sleeps — Orlando makes his way to the forest, where he leaves love-letters on the trees for Rosalind — when the two meet, Rosalind is still disguised as Ganymede, who suggests Orlando unburden himself of his love-sick passion by pretending "he" is Rosalind, making love to "him" and even calling him Rosalind — Oliver appears and tells Rosalind and Aliena that just as he was to be savaged by lions, Orlando, instead of seeking revenge, rescued him and was injured himself — at the sight of the bloody cloth Orlando had asked Oliver to give to the young man posing as Rosalind, Ganymede swoons, causing Oliver to suspects her true identity — Oliver falls in love with Aliena and, converted by Orlando's kindness, offers him his fortune — true identities are revealed and the two happy couples wed — meanwhile Frederick has been converted by a religious man and returns all lands to their rightful owners in exile, who, before leaving the forest, enjoy a final 'rustic revelry'

DRAMATIS PERSONAE

Duke Senior .... an exile in the forest
Rosalind / Ganymede .... his daughter
Lord Amiens ⎫
Lord Jaques ⎭ attending on Duke Senior
Duke Frederick .... Duke Senior's brother
Celia / Aliena................................. his daughter
Oliver ⎫
Orlando ⎬ sons of Sir Rowland de Bois
Jaques ⎭
Adam.............................. aged servant of Oliver
Touchstone...................................... court clown
Sir Oliver Martext .... a vicar
Charles .... a wrestler

Shakespeare wrote this pastoral comedy between 1598 and 1600, and it was first published in the First Folio of 1623. Set in the Forest of Arden, it contrasts town and country.

The Comedy of Errors

Shakespeare's shortest play, written about 1593–4 and first published in the First Folio of 1623, *The Comedy of Errors* was first performed in 1594. Mistaken identities, identical twins, coincidence and slapstick are central features of this fast-paced farce.

> The pleasing punishment that women bear (I, i)
>
> Every why hath a wherefore (II, ii)
>
> Ill deeds are doubled with an evil word (III, ii)

Below: Antipholus of Ephesus attempts to get into his own house, little suspecting that within is his long-lost twin brother. "Let my master in, Luce," cries Dromio of Ephesus. (III, i) But also within, keeping the door, is his own twin brother.

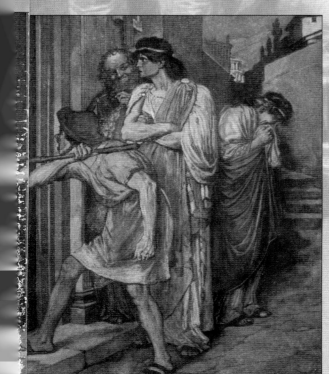

Egeon, a merchant of Syracuse, is discovered in Ephesus — the law prohibits commerce between the two cities, so he must pay a one thousand mark fine or die — Egeon explains that, thirty-three years before, a shipwreck separated his family — he and one of his identical twin babies, Antipholus, and Dromio, a slave baby (also an identical twin) are in Syracuse — now Egeon is desperately searching for his lost family members — who unbeknown to him live in Ephesus — Solinus shows compassion and grants him until sunset to raise money to pay the fine — Antipholus S is also searching in Ephesus, and the local Dromio, Dromio E, mistakes him for his master, Antipholus S, and asks him to hasten home as his wife Adriana awaits him for lunch — Antipholus S tells the local Dromio E not to be ridiculous — he has no wife — and asks him for the thousand marks he entrusted to him earlier — Dromio E believes his master has gone mad and hastens away — Adriana and her sister Luciana come to fetch Antipholus S themselves — bemused, he goes back with them, where Adriana berates him for showing no affection to his wife, and he falls in love with Luciana — further confusions arise involving gold, courtesans and diamonds, causing the visiting Antipholus and his Dromio to seek refuge in a priory and wonder if those of Ephesus are not all witches — Adriana pursues him there, but the Abbess refuses to surrender him — Duke Solinus appears with Egeon and the executioner while the local Antipholus and Dromio petition Solinus for justice — Egeon recognises his long-lost son and servant, but he is so ravaged by grief that they do not recognise him — the Abbess, Antipholus S and Dromio S now emerge, causing utter amazement — the Abbess reveals she is Egeon's long-lost wife Emelia — she tells how, after the shipwreck, a fisherman stole Antipholus E and Dromio E from her — she became a nun, unaware they were still in Ephesus — Solinus pardons Egeon, all confusion is resolved, and Emelia invites everyone to a celebratory feast

DRAMATIS PERSONAE

Solinus.. Duke of Ephesus
Antipholus of Syracuse ⎫
Antipholus of Ephesus ⎭ twins
Egeon .... their father, a Syracuse merchant
Abbess Emelia .... his long-lost wife
Dromio of Syracuse ⎫ .... slave of Antipholus of Syracuse
Dromio of Ephesus ⎭ twins .... slave of Antipholus of Ephesus
Adriana .... wife to Antipholus of Syracuse
Luciana... her sister
Luce / Nell .... servant to Adriana
Balthazar .... a Syracuse merchant
Angelo .... a Syracuse goldsmith

Romeo and Juliet

Above: the balcony scene, where Romeo and Juliet pledge their love.

The Montague and Capulet families have been feuding and fighting in Verona's streets for years — a major brawl causes the Prince of Verona to threaten the respective heads of the two families with execution should further fighting occur — Romeo, Montague's son, is melancholy and admits his unrequited love for Rosaline, Capulet's niece, to his cousin Benvolio — Capulet is holding a masked-ball which will be attended by Rosaline, his daughter Juliet, and Paris, a kinsman of the prince, whom Capulet has invited to court Juliet — Benvolio, hearing of the feast, sneaks in, taking Romeo with him, to show him how many other beauties there are besides Rosaline — Romeo catches sight of Juliet and his heart is lost entirely — he leaves the ball to stand wistfully beneath Juliet's balcony — she appears and whispers his name — emboldened, Romeo reveals himself, and the two exchange vows of love and loyalty — Romeo approaches Friar Lawrence who agrees to marry him to Juliet, secretly in his cell, hoping this may end the families' feuding — the nurse, Juliet's "second mother", gives her the glad news — meanwhile Tybalt, a Capulet and Juliet's cousin, discovers that Romeo was at the ball and challenges him to a duel — Romeo refuses to fight because of his love for Juliet — Mercutio, his dearest friend, takes up the challenge and is killed — distraught and unthinking, Romeo in turn kills Tybalt before fleeing — the prince sentences Romeo to exile — although frenzied with grief when he discovers his sentence, Romeo, with the help of the nurse and the friar, manages to marry Juliet and consummate their love before fleeing to Mantua — attributing Juliet's unhappiness to the death of her cousin Tybalt, her parents arrange for her to marry Paris — initially she refuses but, after consulting with the friar, feigns acceptance — she has agreed to his suggestion that on her marriage eve she take a drug which will render her to seem dead for forty-two hours — Romeo, having been alerted to their plan by a letter from the friar, can be there when she awakes in the family tomb and take her with him to Mantua — but the friar's letter fails to reach Romeo, who hears only the news that Juliet is dead — intending to poison himself, Romeo hurries to her grave, where Paris is grieving bitterly — Paris attempts to arrest Romeo — a fight ensues, and Paris, after asking to be laid beside Juliet, dies — Romeo enters the tomb, places Paris' body within and bids a last unhappy farewell to the apparently dead Juliet — he takes poison and dies — Friar Lawrence, discovering his letter has failed to reach Romeo, rushes to the tomb, arriving just as Juliet awakes — devastated, Juliet drinks the remainder of Romeo's poison and stabs herself with his dagger — the prince and the families are summoned — after hearing the friar's tragic story, the prince, also blaming himself for failing to end the quarrelling, asks Capulet and Montague to witness the results of their feuding — at least for now, the bitterness is ended

DRAMATIS PERSONAE

Romeo . . . . young man of the Montague family
Juliet . . . a young woman of the Capulet family
Nurse . . . . Juliet's confidante
Mercutio . . . . friend to Romeo
Benvolio . . . . cousin to Romeo
Montague Romeo's father, head of the Montagues
Capulet . . Juliet's father, head of the Capulets
Lady Capulet . . . . his wife
Tybalt . . . . Juliet's hot-tempered cousin
Paris . . . . a nobleman suitor to Juliet
Escalus . . . . Prince of Verona
Friar Lawrence . . . . a wise old Franciscan
Balthazar . . . . servant to Romeo

Below: Friar Lawrence's potion. "And this distilled liquor drink thou off ... No warmth, no breath, shall testify thou liv'st; the roses in thy lips and cheeks shall fade to paly ashes; thy eyes' windows fall, like death, when he shuts up the day of life ..." (IV, i)

Left: In despair at the realisation that Romeo is dead, Juliet prepares to take her own life. "O happy dagger! This is thy sheath; there rest, and let me die." (V, iii) At Romeo's feet lies the body of Paris, killed by Romeo.

Above: The two lovers part, he to banishment in Mantua. Juliet: "I must hear from thee every day in the hour, For in a minute there are many days: O by this count I shall be much in years Ere I again behold my Romeo." (III, v)

"

Two households, both alike in dignity / In fair Verona, where we lay our scene / From ancient grudge break to new mutiny, / Where civil blood makes civil hands unclean. / From forth the fatal loins of these two foes A pair of star-cross'd lovers take their life *(Prologue)*

The weakest goes to the wall *(I, i)*

But, soft! what light through yonder window breaks? / It is the east, and Juliet is the sun *(II, i)*

O Romeo, Romeo! wherefore art thou Romeo? *(II, i)*

What's in a name? That which we call a rose / By any other name would smell as sweet *(II, i)*

Good night, good night! parting is such sweet sorrow, / That I shall say good night till it be morrow *(II, i)*

A plague o' both your houses! *(III, i)*

For never was a story of more woe / Than this of Juliet and her Romeo *(V, iii)*

"

Written about 1591–2, *Romeo and Juliet* was first performed between 1594 and 1596 and published in quarto in 1597. It is one of the greatest love stories, and the play has always been very popular, for it has youth, romance, tragedy, violent action and comedy. It also contains some of Shakespeare's most beautiful love poetry.

King Lear

Left: Lear and his fool wander in madness on the windswept heath.

Right: Cordelia's honest answer to the King angers him.

Above: Lear with Cordelia's body, believing to the last that she still lives. "What is't thou say'st? Her voice was ever soft, Gentle and low, an excellent thing in woman." (V, iii)

> Nothing will come of nothing *(I, i)*
>
> How sharper than a serpent's tooth it is / To have a thankless child! *(I, i)*
>
> Blow, winds, and crack your cheeks! rage! blow! / You cataracts and hurricanoes, spout / Till you have drenched our steeples, drowned the cocks ... *(III, ii)*
>
> I am a man / More sinn'd against than sinning *(III, ii)*
>
> O, that way madness lies; let me shun that *(III, iv)*
>
> As flies to wanton boys are we to the gods; / They kill us for their sport ... *(IV, i)*

King Lear, old and weary, decides to divide his kingdom between his three daughters, Goneril, Regan and Cordelia — Lear asks each to declare her love for him — Goneril and Regan flatter him, but Cordelia says only that she loves him as a daughter should — for her honesty, she is banished, and Lear divides the kingdom between Regan and Goneril — Cordelia marries the King of France — the Earl of Goucester has two sons whom he loves equally — but the illegitimate Edmund plots Edgar's downfall so that he can get his father's estates — he forges a letter in which Edgar declares his intent to kill Gloucester, and Edgar is forced to flee for his life and wanders disguised as a madman, "Poor Tom" — Lear and his retinue meantime go to stay with Goneril, but she treats him with contempt and complains his knights are too riotous — Lear, now seeing Goneril's true attitude towards him, curses her and begins a painful self-examination — he leaves for Regan's domain — but the second daughter tells him to apologise to Gonerill and demands he reduce his retinue — grief-stricken at these betrayals, Lear descends to madness, raging naked on a lonely stormy heath, his fool his only companion — they meet "Poor Tom" and Gloucester gives them shelter — Gloucester confides to Edmund that Cordelia is coming with her husband and his French army to rescue Lear — he takes Lear to meet Cordelia at Dover — but Edmund betrays Gloucester, whose eyes are gouged out by Cornwall — Gloucester's servant kills Cornwall — Edgar, in the guise of "Poor Tom", guides Gloucester to Dover and tricks him out of suicide — Lear and Cordelia are reconciled — meanwhile Regan and Goneril become rivals for Edmund's hand, and Albany transfers his loyalties to Lear — in the battle that ensues, both Lear and Cordelia are taken prisoner — Edmund orders them to be hanged — Edgar challenges Edmund to a duel and mortally wounds him — dying, Edmund repents and confesses all — but Cordelia is already dead — Goneril poisons Regan so she may have Edmund — and when she discovers he is dead she kills herself — now Lear enters carrying Cordelia's body — he dies, a broken old man, with the only daughter who loved him — Gloucester is reconciled with Edgar — and Albany takes power

King Lear was written about 1605, probably first performed two years later and printed in a quarto edition in 1608. One of the greatest of all tragedies, it is an immensely powerful and disturbing play, and is seen as a benchmark role for leading actors.

DRAMATIS PERSONAE

King Lear	King of Ancient Britain
Goneril	his eldest daughter
Albany	her husband
Regan	Lear's second daughter
Cornwall	her husband
Cordelia	Lear's youngest daughter
Gloucester	loyal friend of the King
Edgar (Tom)	his eldest son)
Edmund	Gloucester's younger, illegitimate son
Kent	a nobleman loyal to the King
Fool	Lear's court jester
Oswald	Goneril's steward

Left: Othello has slain Desdemona. "The Moor is of a free and open nature, That thinks men honest That but seem to be so; And will as tenderly be led by the nose ..." (I, iii)

Othello
The Moor of Venice

Written around 1603–4, *Othello* was first performed at court in 1604 and published in quarto in 1622. Fast-paced, jealousy is the principal theme.

> I will wear my heart upon my sleeve / For daws to peck at *(I, i)*
>
> How poor are they that have not patience! *(II, iii)*
>
> O beware, my lord, of jealousy! / It is the green-eyed monster, which doth mock / The meat it feeds on *(III, iii)*
>
> Trifles light as air / Are to the jealous confirmations strong / As proofs of holy writ *(III, iii)*

Othello promotes Cassio to be his lieutenant over the ambitious Iago, who is now bent on revenge — Othello also secretly marries Desdemona, daughter of a Venetian senator — Roderigo, Iago's friend, who is in love with Desdemona, is heartbroken — in Cyprus, Iago begins his machinations — he tells Roderigo that Cassio is in love with Desdemona and encourages him to pick a fight with him — at a feast, Cassio, who has no head for drink, is encouraged to imbibe too much by Iago — Roderigo provokes Cassio and they fight — his reputation destroyed, Cassio faces demotion by Othello — Iago suggests he ask Desdemona to speak in his defence and arranges for Othello to observe the conversation — thus planting the first seeds of jealousy in the Moor's mind — when Desdemona presses Cassio's cause, Othello's suspicions grow — Iago tricks his wife, Emilia, into stealing a precious handkerchief given to Desdemona by Othello — Iago plants it in Cassio's chamber, and he in turn gives it to his mistress, Bianca — Iago tells Othello he saw Cassio wiping his beard with it — when Othello asks Desdemona where his gift is, she explains that it is lost — this all feeds Othello's suspicions — Iago lets Othello hear Cassio talking irreverently about Bianca but lets him believe Cassio speaks of Desdemona — enraged, Othello orders Iago to kill Cassio and confronts Desdemona, who protests her innocence and is vindicated by Emilia — Iago persuades Roderigo to kill Cassio, persuading him that Desdemona will then be his — but Roderigo deals Cassio only a superficial wound, and in the commotion Iago, fearful of betrayal, kills Roderigo — hearing the noise, Othello (believing Cassio dead) strangles Desdemona — Othello explains to Emilia that she was sleeping with Cassio and says Iago will confirm this — Emoilia now understands all and confesses to stealing the handkerchief — Othello slays her — Cassio explains Iago's schemes to Othello who, overcome with shame and grief, kills himself — Iago's fate is to be decided in Venice

DRAMATIS PERSONAE

Othello	a Moor in the service of Venice
Desdemona	his bride
Brabantio	her father, a Venetian senator
Gratiano	his brother
Iago	Othello's trusted ensign
Emilia	his wife, Desdemona's attendant
Cassio	Othello's lieutenant
Bianca	his mistress, a courtesan of Cyprus
Roderigo	jealous suitor of Desdemona
Lodovico	kinsman to Brabantio
Clown	servant to Othello
Montano	governor of Cyprus
Duke of Venice	

The Merchant of Venice

Right: Shylock's courtroom triumph is short-lived. "This bond doth give thee here no jot of blood; the words expressly are 'a pound of flesh': Take then thy bond, take thou thy pound of flesh; But, in the cutting it, if thou dost shed One drop of Christian blood ..." (IV, i)

Written about 1596–8 and published in a quarto edition in 1600, its first recorded performance was at court five years later. Controversial in its anti-Semitism, it features a "stock character" Jew in Shylock, who can also be played in a sympathetic light.

Shylock bears a grudge against Antonio, who frequently insults him in public — Antony has a friend, Bassanio, who needs 3,000 ducats to help press his suit for Portia, a rich heiress of Belmont — as he is expecting several ships bearing merchandise to arrive shortly, Antonio confidently agrees to stand surety — even though Shylock says surety shall not be financial but a pound of Antonio's flesh — Antonio agrees — Portia's late father has made a condition of her marriage that suitors choose correctly from a gold, silver and lead casket or lose their suit — many illustrious gentlemen, none to Portia's taste, have already failed this text — Bassanio arrives in Belmont and finds favour in Portia's eyes — by means of music she alludes subtly to which casket Bassanio should choose — and he correctly chooses the lead casket, finding within a portrait of Portia — she gives him a ring but warns him that if he loses it he will also lose her love — meanwhile Shylock's daughter Jessica has fallen in love with a Christian, Lorenzo — they elope with her jewels — now comes catastrophic news: Antonio's ships have sunk — Bassanio marries Portia and rushes to his friend's side — it is too late, for the terms of the surety have become due — Portia, unbeknown to Bassanio, also departs to Venice, where by disguise she becomes Antonio's defence lawyer, "Balthazar" — she argues persuasively, but the judge has no option but to agree with Shylock's right to claim the flesh. 'Balthazar' now tells Shylock that, although he may take the flesh, he may not take one drop of blood — the terms of the contract specify that if he should take more or less than exactly one pound of flesh, Shylock must himself be put to death — realising this is impossible, Shylock says he will accept the 3,000 ducats — but it is too late — for plotting the death of a citizen he must forfeit his goods and convert to Christianity — Bassanio asks 'Balthazar' what he wants for saving Antonio's life — 'Balthazar' asks for Bassanio's wedding ring, which he reluctantly surrenders — reunited, Bassanio and Portia quarrel over the loss of the ring until she admits her subterfuge and produces it — and finally it is discovered that three of Antonio's ships have arrived in port

DRAMATIS PERSONAE

Duke of Venice
Shylock .... a Jewish moneylender
Jessica .... his daughter
Launcelot Gobbo .... servant to Shylock
Old Gobbo .... his father
Tubal .... Jewish friend to Shylock
Antonio .... a merchant
Bassanio .... his friend
Gratiano
Salarino ⎫ friends to Bassanio and Antonio
Salanio ⎭
Portia .... a wealthy heiress
Nerissa .... her lady in waiting
Balthazar ⎫ servants to Portia
Stephano ⎭
Lorenzo .... in love with Jessica

© THIRD MILLENNIUM PRESS LTD, 2005

" Signor Antonio, many a time and oft / In the Rialto you have rated me / About my moneys and my usances: / Still have I borne it with a patient shrug, / For sufferance is the badge of all our tribe. / You call me misbeliever, cut-throat dog / And spit upon my Jewish gabardine / And all for use of that which is mine own *(I, iii)*

The quality of mercy is not strain'd, / It droppeth as the gentle rain from heaven / Upon the place beneath: it is twice blest; / It blesseth him that gives and him that takes *(IV, i)* "

The Two Gentlemen of Verona

" Experience is by industry achieved / And perfected by the swift course of time *(I, iii)*

That man that hath a tongue, I say, is no man, / If with his tongue he cannot win a woman *(III, i)* "

DRAMATIS PERSONAE

The Duke of Milan
Silvia .... his daughter
Julia .... betrothed to Proteus
Lucetta .... her servant
Proteus ..... a gentleman of Verona
Antonio .... his father
Panthino .... his servant
Launce .... Proteus' servant
Crab .... his dog
Valentine ... a gentleman of Verona
Speed .... his page
Thurio ... a suitor for Silvia's hand
Sir Eglamour .... a gentleman
Host .... an innkeeper

Valentine, restless, departs to Milan where he is a guest of its duke — he asks Proteus to join him, but Proteus is reluctant to leave Julia — he is finally ordered by his father to join Valentine, who recommends him highly to the Duke — Valentine, meanwhile, has fallen in love with Silvia, and she returns his affections — but she is betrothed to Thurio, an older courtier — Valentine and Silvia decide to elope, and he confides his plans to Proteus — but Proteus has also fallen in love with Silvia — he debates briefly the consequences of betraying Valentine to the Duke — he will lose not only Julia but his oldest friend — eventually he decides to put himself first — Proteus pretends to be devastated when Valentine tells him the Duke has banished him — Valentine leaves for the surrounding forests and becomes leader of an outlaw gang — with Valentine gone, the Duke assures Thurio that his suit will now be taken seriously — and meanwhile a grief-stricken Silvia is kept under house arrest — Julia, missing Proteus, disguises herself as "Sebastian" and arrives in Milan in time to hear Proteus tell Silvia that Julia is dead — unmoved, Silvia continues to reject him before escaping to the forest, where she is captured by Valentine's men — before they can take her to him, she is "rescued" by Proteus who is accompanied by "Sebastian" among others — while Valentine watches unnoticed, Silvia continues to reject Proteus who now threatens to ravish her — Valentine reveals himself and challenges Proteus, who asks for forgiveness — Valentine grants this, even offering Silvia to Proteus, which causes an overwrought "Sebastian" to faint momentarily — she reveals herself to be Julia, and Proteus declares himself delighted to see her again — the Duke and Thurio now arrive, having been apprehended by Valentine's men — challenged by Valentine, Thurio renounces his claim to Silvia — Julia and Proteus are reconciled — the Duke agrees to a match between Valentine and Silvia and, at Valentine's request, pardons his outlaws

One of Shakespeare's earliest plays, this was written 1590–1, and first published in 1623 in the First Folio. The themes are friendship, loyalty, betrayal, and love.

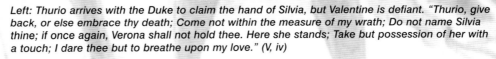

Left: Thurio arrives with the Duke to claim the hand of Silvia, but Valentine is defiant. "Thurio, give back, or else embrace thy death; Come not within the measure of my wrath; Do not name Silvia thine; if once again, Verona shall not hold thee. Here she stands; Take but possession of her with a touch; I dare thee but to breathe upon my love." (V, iv)

A Midsummer Night's Dream

Written 1594–6; first published 1600; first performance at court 1604 but performed in public several times before this

Below: "I know a bank where the wild thyme blows, Where oxlips and the nodding violet grows, Quite over-canopied with luscious woodbine, With sweet musk-roses, and with eglantine." (II, i)

DRAMATIS PERSONAE

Theseus	Duke of Athens
Hippolyta	Amazon queen he has conquered
Philostrate	Master of the Revels
Egeus	father to Hermia
Hermia	his daughter
Lysander	in love with Hermia
Helena	Hermia's friend, in love with Demetrius
Demetrius	betrothed to Hermia
Oberon	King of the Fairies
Titania	Queen of the Fairies
Puck (Robin Goodfellow)	goblin in Oberon's service
Peaseblossom, Cobweb, Moth and Mustardseed	fairy attendants to Titania
Nick Bottom	a weaver (*Pyramus)
Peter Quince	a carpenter (*Thisbe's father)
Francis Flute	a bellows-mender (*Thisbe)
Tom Snout	a tinker (*Wall)
Snug	a Joiner (*Lion)
Robin Starveling	a tailor (*Moonshine)

* (Parts taken in the play *Pyramus and Thisbe*)

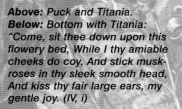

Above: Puck and Titania.
Below: Bottom with Titania: "Come, sit thee down upon this flowery bed, While I thy amiable cheeks do coy, And stick musk-roses in thy sleek smooth head, And kiss thy fair large ears, my gentle joy. (IV, i)

Theseus and Hippolyta are planning for their wedding — they are visited by Egeus — his daughter, Hermia, wants to marry her lover, Lysander, instead of Egeus' choice, Demetrius — the Duke adjudicates: she must marry according to her father's wishes or enter a nunnery – or face death — she has four days to decide — Hermia meets Lysander in the forest to elope — meanwhile a group of artisans meet to discuss the play they hope to perform at their lord's wedding — they agree to reconvene in the woods to rehearse — In the forest, Oberon and Titania are quarrelling — to win the argument, Oberon sends Puck to find the magic juice from a special flower, which will make the recipient fall in love with whomever he or she first sees on waking —Helena has told Demetrius that Hermia and Lysander are fleeing, and they now follow them through the forest — Oberon overhears Demetrius's rejection of Helena's affections — to punish him, Oberon tells Puck to use the love potion on him so he will fall for Helena — and when Titania is asleep Oberon also drops the love potion upon her eyes — Hermia and Lysander arrive and settle down to sleep — Puck, mistaking Lysander for Demetrius, puts the love potion in his eyes —Lysander wakens at the arrival of Helena, falls in love with her and chases after her — The would-be thespians arrive and begin their rehearsal — Puck, as a practical joke, casts a spell on Bottom, giving him the head of an ass — the other players flee while Bottom, unaware of his altered countenance, sings to keep his spirits up — this wakes Titania, who, upon seeing him, immediately falls in love — she leads him to her bower — Puck reports to Oberon, who is delighted at Titania's situation with Bottom; but less happy to find that Puck has mistaken his other victim — so Oberon puts the love-potion on Demetrius' eyes and gets Puck to bring Helena so that she is Demetrius' first sight on awakening; he duly wakes and falls in love with her — Helena, now wooed by both Demetrius and Lysander, thinks they are making fun of her and that her friend Hermia is in on the scheme — Hermia thinks Helena has stolen Lysander from her; they quarrel while Lysander and Demetrius depart to fight a duel — on Oberon's orders, Puck separates them all and releases Lysander from his spell — Oberon undoes the spell he put on Titania — and Puck changes Bottom's head back into human form — Oberon and Titania are reconciled — Theseus, Hippolyta and Egeus arrive — the lovers awake and Theseus reverses his judgement: when the royal marriage takes place, Hermia and Lysander may marry; so too Helena and Demetrius — the four lovers think they are dreaming and return with Theseus and Hippolyta to the palace — Bottom too thinks he has been dreaming — Theseus and Hippolyta discuss these strange occurrences — then he selects Bottom and his friends to perform their play, *Pyramus and Thisbe*, at the wedding celebration — this they do, with amateur incompetence, but all enjoy themselves — the newly-weds retire to bed, then the fairies arrive to bless them — and Puck delivers an epilogue

Written 1594–6, *A Midsummer Night's Dream* was first published in 1600. Its first performance at court was in 1604, but it was performed in public several times before this

> **❝** The course of true love never did run smooth *(I, i)*
>
> Love looks not with the eyes, but with the mind, / And therefore is winged Cupid painted blind *(I, i)*
>
> I'll speak in a monstrous little voice *(I, ii)*
>
> I must go seek some dew-drops here, / And hang a pearl in every cowslip's ear *(II, i)*
>
> Ill met by moonlight, proud Titania *(II, i)*
>
> I'll put a girdle round the earth / In forty minutes *(II, i)*
>
> Bless thee, Bottom! bless thee! thou art translated *(III, i)*
>
> Lord, what fools these mortals be! *(III, ii)*
>
> Thus die I, thus, thus, thus. / Now am I dead, / Now am I fled; / My soul is in the sky: / Tongue lose thy light; / Moon take thy flight: / Now die, die, die, die, die *(V, i)*
>
> Asleep, my love? / What, dead, my dove? / O Pyramus, arise! *(V, i)* **❞**

Left: Lysander, under Puck's spell, tells Helena he loves her. Helena: "Good troth, you do me wrong, good sooth you do – In such distainful manner me to woo." (II, ii)

Right: The fairies leave Bottom with his head restored to its normal aspect. He awakes: "I have had a dream, past the wit of man to say what dream it was ..." (IV, i)

Macbeth

Written in 1606, *Macbeth* received its first recorded performance in 1611 but was not published until the First Folio of 1623. One of Shakespeare's bloodiest dramas, it is an emotionally intense play, traditionally associated with bad luck.

Macbeth defeats a traitorous Scot, the Thane of Cawdor — with his friend Banquo, he is leaving the battlefield when they are accosted by three witches — they predict that Macbeth will become Thane of Cawdor, then King of Scotland — and that Banquo will not be a king but that his children will be — their disbelief is confounded when King Duncan confers the title Thane of Cawdor upon Macbeth — who begins to harbour ambitions — Lady Macbeth urges Macbeth to murder Duncan and seize the throne — with grave doubts, he agrees — Duncan and his retinue come to Macbeth's castle as guests — Macbeth has his opportunity, but yet has second thoughts — his wife calls him a coward: he must enter Duncan's chamber at midnight and kill him with his servant's daggers, while they lie drugged and unconscious — thus goaded, Macbeth carries out the murder — but he forgets to leave behind the murder weapons to incriminate the servants — overwrought, he refuses to return to the chamber, and Lady Macbeth takes the daggers back herself, getting blood on her hands in the process — Macduff discovers the murdered Duncan, at which Macbeth and his wife feign horror — Macbeth and Macduff visit the bed chamber, and a hysterical Macbeth kills Duncan's servants, saying afterwards that it was not safe to let them live — Duncan's elder son Malcolm flees, fearing for his life, and Macbeth is named king — Macbeth now recalls the witches' prophecy that Banquo's children should be kings — clearly Banquo and his son Fleance must die if his own children are to inherit the crown — Macbeth's inept assassins kill Banquo, but Fleance escapes — Macbeth is devastated — at his coronation feast he sees Banquo's ghost, whom he constantly addresses to the consternation of all, until Lady Macbeth forces him to leave — he resolves to assassinate Macduff, who was absent and is surely harbouring traitorous intent — first, however, he consults the witches — they tell him that "none of woman born" can harm him, that he must "beware Macduff", and that he is safe until Birnam Wood comes to his castle — discovering Macduff has fled to England, Macbeth has his wife and son murdered — when news reaches Macduff, who now, together with Malcolm and the King of England, is planning war against Macbeth, he vows a terrible vengeance — meanwhile Lady Macbeth descends into madness, wracked with guilt and walking in her sleep, trying to wash blood from her hands — eventually she kills herself — now Macbeth and his army prepare to fight the English — and he seems to see Birnam Wood coming closer to his castle — Malcolm has ordered his men each to cut down a branch and carry it in front of them to create confusion — convinced he is invulnerable, Macbeth fights on — but his nemesis, Macduff, who came into the world by Caesarian section, not "born of woman", deals him the fatal blow — and Malcolm is proclaimed King of Scotland

Above: Macbeth hesitates to carry out the murder of Duncan. MACBETH: *"If we should fail,–"* LADY MACBETH: *"We fail. But screw your courage to the sticking place, And we'll not fail." (I, vi)*

Above: Lady Macbeth waits and listens as her husband carries out the foul deed. "Alack! I am afraid they have awak'd. And 'tis not done; the attempt and not the deed confounds us ..." (II, ii)

Left: The ghost of Banquo enters and sits in Macbeth's place. MACBETH: *"Avaunt! and quit my sight! let the earth hide thee! Thy bones are marrowless, thy blood is cold; Thou hast no speculation in those eyes Which thou dost glare with." (III, iv)*

Above: The weird sisters who predict the fates of Macbeth and Banquo. "Double, double toil and trouble; | Fire burn and cauldron bubble ..." (IV, i)

66

When shall we three meet again / In thunder, lightning, or in rain? / When the hurlyburly's done / When the battle's lost and won (I, i)

If it were done when 'tis done, then 'twere well / It were done quickly (I, vii)

Is this a dagger which I see before me, / The handle toward my hand? Come let me clutch thee. / I have thee not, and yet I see thee still. / Art thou not, fatal vision, sensible / To feeling as to sight? Or art thou but / A dagger of the mind, a false creation, / Proceeding from the heat-oppressed brain? (II, i)

There's daggers in men's smiles (II, iii)

By the pricking of my thumbs, / Something wicked this way comes (IV, i)

Out, damned spot! out, I say! (V, i)

To-morrow, and to-morrow, and to-morrow, / Creeps in this petty pace from day to day, / To the last syllable of recorded time, / And all our yesterdays have lighted fools / The way to dusty death. Out, out, brief candle! / Life's but a walking shadow, a poor player, / That struts and frets his hour upon the stage, / And then is heard no more: it is a tale / Told by an idiot, full of sound and fury, / Signifying nothing (V, v)

99

DRAMATIS PERSONAE

Macbeth .... a general in the King's army
Lady Macbeth .... his wife
Banquo .... a fellow general in the King's army
Fleance .... his son
Duncan .... King of Scotland
Malcolm .... his elder son
Donalbain .... Duncan's second son
Macduff ⎫
Lennox ⎪
Ross ⎬ Scottish noblemen
Menteith ⎪
Angus ⎪
Caithness ⎭
Siward .... Earl of Northumberland
Young Siward .... his son
The Three Witches .... prophets of Macbeth's fate

Above: Lady Macbeth sleepwalks, on her way to madness and death. "Lo you! here she comes. This is her very guise; and, upon my life, fast asleep ..." (V, i)

Julius Caesar

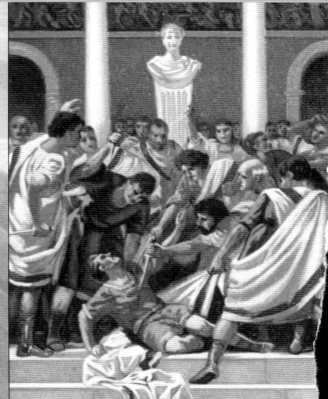

Right: The assassination of Caesar. CASCA: *"Speak, hands, for me!"* CAESAR: *"Et tu, Brute? Then fall, Caesar!"* CINNA: *"Liberty! Freedom! Tyranny is dead!" (III, i) But, crucially, they fail to kill Mark Antony.*

Caesar arrives victorious in Rome — a soothsayer tells him to "beware the Ides of March", but Caesar dismisses him — his friend, Mark Antony, in front of the mob, offers him the crown three times, but each time Caesar refuses — meanwhile, Brutus, a friend of Caesar but also an idealistic republican, is persuaded by Cassius, jealous of Caesar's triumph, to conspire with him against Caesar — they fear that Caesar will become a tyrant — Brutus, however, refuses to have Antony killed as well — Calpurnia, Caesar's wife, dreams he is murdered and begs him not to go to the Senate — Artemidorus tries to warns him of the conspiracy but is ignored — Caesar enters the Forum on the fateful Ides and is stabbed to death by Brutus, Cassius and five other conspirators — Antony shakes the killers' hands but asks as an old friend if he may speak at Caesar's funeral — Brutus, against Cassius' advice, agrees — with clever rhetoric, Mark Antony whips up the crowd in support of the murdered man — Brutus and Cassius flee Rome, leaving power in the hands of Antony, Octavius and Lepidus — meanwhile Cassius and Brutus prepare for war, while Mark Antony and his forces march to Philippi — there battle is joined — while Antony is winning against Cassius, Brutus is succeeding against Octavius — Cassius, thinking all is lost, kills himself — and when Brutus discovers this, he too despairs and falls on his sword — when Antony hears this, he admits that Brutus was truly noble and alone of the assassins acted for the common good — Octavius orders his honourable funeral

Left: Caesar's wife Calpurnia tries to prevent Caesar attending the Senate, having had portentous dreams. On his way, Caesar will again be warned: "Beware the Ides of March." (I, i)

DRAMATIS PERSONAE

Julius Caesar .... Rome's great general
Calpurnia... his wife
Octavius Caesar .... his nephew and heir
Mark Antony ....Caesar's friend and lieutenant
Brutus.. a senator
Portia.. his wife
Cassius, Cinna, Casca,
Metellus Cimber, Trebonius, } conspirators
Ligarius, Decius Brutus } against Caesar
Cicero, Publius, Popilius Lena .... senators
Artemidorus .... a soothsayer
Cinna .... a poet
Lepidus........... third member of the triumvirate

> Why, man, he doth bestride the narrow world / Like a Colossus ... *(I, ii)*

Let me have about me men that are fat; / Sleek-headed men and such as sleep o' nights. / Yond Cassius has a lean and hungry look; / He thinks too much: such men are dangerous *(I, ii)*

Friends, Romans, countrymen, lend me your ears; / I come to bury Caesar, not to praise him *(III, ii)*

Written about 1599 and first performed that same year, *Julius Caesar* was first published in the 1623 First Folio. The tragic hero is the inflexibly idealistic Brutus.

Antony and Cleopatra

© THIRD MILLENNIUM PRESS LTD. 2005

This was written about 1606, and published in the First Folio of 1623, but there is no record of its being performed during Shakespeare's lifetime. The conflict at the heart of the play is for Antony's soul.

> Age cannot wither her, nor custom stale Her infinite variety *(II, ii)*

The barge she sat in, like a burnish'd throne, / Burn'd on the water; the poop was beaten gold; / Purple the sails, and so perfumed that / The winds were lovesick with them; the oars were silver, / Which to the tune of flutes kept stroke ... *(II, ii)*

Left and below: The battle of Actium and its consequence. Cleopatra leaves the battle prematurely and Antony follows. "... Antony, Claps on his sea-wing, and like a doting mallard, Leaving the fight in height, flies after her. I never saw an action of such shame ..." (III, ix) Below: The lovers back at Alexandria. ANTONY: *"I have offended reputation. A most unnoble swerving ... O! whither hast thou led me, Egypt?" (III, xi)*

Mark Antony, Octavius Caesar and Lepidus rule the Roman world — Antony, however, has abandoned Rome and his wife Fulvia for Egypt and the charms of seductive Cleopatra — Antony's wife dies and Antony returns to Rome — Octavius and Antony bury their differences, and Antony agrees to marry Octavius's sister, Octavia, to cement their alliance — Cleopatra is furious, jealous and humiliated — Antony is in Athens with Octavia where he is told that Octavius is speaking ill of him to the Senate — he asks Octavia to choose between him and her brother — when she is unable to do so, Antony returns to Egypt, where he declares Cleopatra queen of parts of the Roman empire and her son by Julius Caesar a king — war between Octavius and Antony erupts — they fight at sea, but Cleopatra's navy is no match for Octavius' and flees — Antony petitions Octavius to recognise Cleopatra's dynasty and let him live with her — but Caesar, will only recognise Cleopatra's title if she gives up Antony — Antony returns to battle — Cleopatra's navy surrenders without fighting — believing himself betrayed, Antony rails against her wildly — fearing for her life, she hides in her tomb and lets him think she has killed herself but that her last words were of him — Antony falls on his sword — as he lies bleeding, he learns Cleopatra is still alive and is taken to her tomb, where he dies romantically in her arms — Octavius pays tribute to Antony's greatness and regrets sincerely his passing and their rift — Cleopatra, who refuses to bow to Octavius, learns then that her fate is to be paraded through Rome — unable to bear such humiliation, she allows poisonous asps to bite her — and Octavius buries her beside Antony

DRAMATIS PERSONAE

Mark Antony } triumvirs,
Octavius Caesar } rulers of Rome
M. Aemilius Lepidus }
Cleopatra .... Queen of Egypt
Sextus Pompeius .... son of Pompey the Great
Octavia..................... sister to Octavius Caesar
Charmian, Iras...............attendants to Cleopatra
Taurus .... Octavius' lieutenant
Canidius ....Antony's lieutenant

Twelfth Night
Or, What You Will

Written in 1599–1600, this was probably first performed in 1601 and appears in the First Folio of 1623. One of Shakespeare's greatest comedies, it is set on the last night of the Christmas revels, which befits its ingredients of disguises and jollity.

66 If music be the food of love, play on *(I, i)*

I am sure care's an enemy to life *(I, iii)*

Many a good hanging prevents a bad marriage *(I, v)*

O time! Thou must untangle this, not I; / It is too hard a knot for me to untie! *(II, ii)*

In my stars I am above thee; but be not afraid of greatness; some are born great, some achieve greatness, and some have greatness thrust upon 'em *(II, v)* 99

Viola and Sebastian are shipwrecked on the shores of Illyria each believing the other dead — fascinated by her father's descriptions of Duke Orsino, whose court is nearby, Viola disguised as a boy, Cesario, determines to become his page — very soon, she feels the stirrings of love — Orsino, however, is in love with Olivia — but she tells him she is in mourning for her dead brother and is not considering suitors — Orsino sends Cesario to plead his case with Olivia — and Olivia promptly falls in love with Cesario — meanwhile Sebastian is rescued by Antonio, on old enemy of Orsino's, and he too makes his way to Orsino's court — Sir Toby Belch has persuaded Sir Andrew Aguecheek to support him, by making him believe Olivia is interested in marrying him — Sir Toby presses Sir Andrew to challenge Cesario to a duel — as the unwilling combatants prepare, Antonio comes upon the scene — believing Cesario to be Sebastian, he intervenes but is arrested by Orsino's men — Cesario does not recognise Antonio, who is dismayed at this slight — Aguecheek and Belch now come across Sebastian and, believing him to be Cesario, again challenge him — combat ensues, Sebastian winning until Olivia, also believing him to be Cesario, stops the fighting — she proposes marriage to "Cesario" — bemused, but delighted, since he has fallen in love with Olivia, Sebastian agrees — Antonio is taken before Orsino for questioning — Cesario tells him that Antonio rescued her, and Antonio insists that he also rescued Cesario from the shipwreck — Olivia now arrives, looking for her new husband, and is distraught and mystfied when Cesario prepares to leave with Orsino — Belch and Aguecheek arrive to complain they have been injured by Cesario, who is vehemently denying the charge just as Sebastian arrives and apologises to Olivia for hurting her kinsman — Sebastian and Viola recognise one another and are reunited — Cesario, now revealed as the lovely Viola, prompts Orsino to pledge his love for her, which is fulsomely returned, while Sebastian and Olivia remain happily married

DRAMATIS PERSONAE

Orsino......................... Duke of Illyria
Viola / Cesario.......... a young woman
Sebastian .. her long lost twin brother
Antonio ...... his friend, a sea captain
Olivia .... a wealthy lady
Malvolio .... her steward
Feste........ a clown in Olivia's service
Sir Toby Belch........... uncle to Olivia
Sir Andrew Aguecheek ...... his friend
Maria .... servant to Olivia

Above: Viola, disguised as Cesario, with Olivia, who falls in love with the page. When all disguises are revealed, she finds her true love, Viola's twin brother Sebastian.

The Taming of the Shrew

A play within a play, *The Taming of the Shrew* was written early in the 1590s and published in the First Folio of 1623. Set in Padua, it deals with the contemporary domination of women by their fathers and husbands, and the undermining of this.

66 Come, madam wife, sit by my side and let the world slip: we shall ne'er be younger *(Introduction, i)*

There's small choice in rotten apples *(I, i)*

Who wooed in haste, and means to wed at leisure *(III, ii)* 99

DRAMATIS PERSONAE

Baptista Minola .... a nobleman of Padua
Katherina (Kate) } his daughters
Bianca
Hortensio / Litio................ suitor to Bianca
Petruchio................ his friend, from Verona
Grumio .... his servant
Lucentio / Cambio....... a student from Pisa
Tranio } his servants
Biondello
Vincentio .... Lucentio's father

Left: Kate hits Petruchio who tells her: "Thus in plain terms: your father hath consented That you shall be my wife; your dowry 'greed on; And will you, nill you, I will marry you." (II, i)

Ill-tempered Kate and her lovely sister Bianca are daughters of wealthy Paduan merchant, Baptista — Lucentio arrives to study at university and falls in love with Bianca — determined to get closer to her, he changes clothes with Tranio and offers his services as a poetry tutor named "Cambio" — her other suitors are Hortensio, who disguises himself as "Litio" a music tutor, Grumio a rich, capering old man, and Tranio, who presents himself as his master Lucentio — Baptista declares that none may marry Bianca until shrewish Kate is wed — Hortensio's old friend, care-free Petruchio, is attracted by Kate's fortune and declares he will both marry and tame her — outrageously late for his wedding, he causes Kate to wail, as she realises she no longer wants to be alone — Petruchio constantly contradicts Kate, calling the sun the moon, refuses her food and sleep until she agrees with all he says — eventually exhausted, Kate becomes a devoted wife — Baptista declares Bianca's hand may be claimed by the wealthiest suitor, "Lucentio", in reality Lucentio's servant Tranio, so long as guarantees of his dowry arrive from his father Vincentio — meanwhile "Cambio" reveals he is really Lucentio, and Bianca is charmed by his suit — "Litio" has less success, while Hortensio abandons his courtship and marries a pleasing widow — Tranio persuades a schoolmaster to impersonate Vincentio, and he "guarantees" "Lucentio's" dowry to Bianca's father — Cambio is sent to tell Bianca to prepare with haste for her nuptials — meanwhile the real Vincentio arrives in Padua to see Lucentio just as Cambio is marrying Bianca and is turned away from the church by the false Vincentio — the real Vincentio is outraged, as is Baptista when he discovers that Bianca is married to Cambio not "Lucentio" — all is finally revealed, but Vincentio and Baptista remain angry at being duped — Hortensio, Lucentio and Petruchio wager upon whose wife will be the most obedient — when they send for them, only Kate arrives — Hortensio and Lucentio marvel at this miracle

Much Ado About Nothing

Left: Beatrice overhears Hero, Ursula and Margaret discussing Beatrice's passion for Benedick. BEATRICE: *"What fire is in mine ears? Can this be true? Stand I condemn'd for pride and scorn so much? Contempt, farewell! and maiden pride adieu! No glory lives behind the back of such. And, Benedick, love on; I will requite thee ..." (III, i)*

Claudio is a war hero in the army of Don Pedro, Prince of Arragon, which has just vanquished that of his villainous brother Don John — he arrives at the Court of Leonato, Governor of Messina, with Lord Benedick, and John who superficially appears to be reconciled with Pedro — Claudio falls in love with Leonato's daughter, Hero — Benedick conducts an ascerbic, but light-hearted, relationship with Beatrice, Leonato's niece, neither admitting their attraction for the other — an evening's masked revelry is about to commence — Pedro offers to disguise himself as Claudio and woo Hero, on Claudio's behalf — the still resentful John, aware of this, sees a way to best at least one of Pedro's upstarts — recognising Claudio beneath his mask, John tells him that Pedro is in love with Hero — Claudio believes him, but Pedro's matchmaking has been a success — Leonato promises Hero to Claudio, and doubt vanishes — enraged, John hatches a plan whereby his heavily bribed servant, Borachio, will dally with his real paramour, Margaret, who unknowingly will look like Hero — John invites Pedro and Claudio to observe the "unfaithful" Hero, and both are duped — they leave the midnight scene, but constable Dogberry appears and hears Borachio discuss their trick and arrests them — meanwhile Leonato, Pedro and Claudio, matchmaking for Beatrice and Benedick, purposefully let Benedick overhear discussion of Beatrice's vehement passion for him — Benedick now realises that he too loves Beatrice — Hero, who is also privy to the plot, stages a conversation which Beatrice overhears, in which Benedick is praised and Beatrice described as too in love with herself to love another — mortified, Beatrice resolves to return Benedick's love — Claudio attends his wedding ceremony the next day, as planned, but rejects Hero at the altar — Leonato is eventually convinced of his daughter's unfaithfulness by the deceived Pedro and the deceitful John — Hero faints — Friar Francis, who was conducting the ceremony, believes in Hero's innocence and devises a plan — when Claudio stormed out of the church, Hero appeared dead — so, Friar Francis suggests, they pretend Hero really is dead — then Claudio would realise that she must truly be innocent — meanwhile Benedict and Beatrice finally confess their love for one another — Benedick, as token of his love for her, promises to challenge Claudio to a duel for so humiliating Hero — Claudio is devastated when Benedict does so — however, he begins to become suspicious when Benedick mentions that John has fled Messina — Constable Dogberry meanwhile produces Borachio, who confesses publicly and reveals John as the architect of the piece — Benedick proposes marriage to Beatrice — Claudio and Pedro ask Leonato what they can do to atone for Hero's death — he says Claudio must read an epitaph over Hero's "grave" and then marry Hero's cousin — he agrees wholeheartedly to this — the mysterious masked woman in the church is, of course, Hero — after some final verbal sparring, Benedick and Beatrice publicly admit their love — Benedick and Claudio are reconciled and, as the feasting begins, news reaches Messina that John has been captured

© THIRD MILLENNIUM PRESS LTD, 2005

DRAMATIS PERSONAE

Leonato	Governor of Messina
Hero	his beautiful daughter
Beatrice	Leonato's adopted niece
Antonio	Leonato's elder brother
Don Pedro	Prince of Arragon
Don John	his illegitimate brother
Borachio } Conrade }	his servants
Benedick	a soldier, friend to Don Pedro
Margaret	Hero's maid
Ursula	a servingwoman to Hero
Claudio	a young soldier
Dogberry	Constable of Messina
Verges	his assistant
Friar Francis	a monk

Considered one of Shakespeare's best comedies, *Much Ado About Nothing* was written abut 1598 and published in quarto two years later, having already been performed. At its centre is the battle between the sexes, enlivened with plenty of tricks, intrigues and verbal sparring.

Left: Benedick and Beatrice confess their mutual love. BENEDICK: *"I do love nothing in the world so well as you: is not that strange?"* BEATRICE: *As strange as the thing I know not. It were as possible for me to say I loved nothing as well as you ..." (IV, i)*

Above: Hero reveals her true identity to Claudio. CLAUDIO: *"Sweet, let me see your face."* LEON *"No, that you shall not, till you take her hand Before this friar, and swear to marry her."* CLAUDIO: *"Give me your hand: before this holy friar, I am your husband, if you like of me."* HERO: *"And when I liv'd, I was your other wife: (unmasking) And when you lov'd , you were my other husband."* CLAUDIO: *"Another Hero!"* HERO: *"Nothing certainer: One Hero died defil'd, but I do live, And surely as I live, I am a maid." (V, iv)*

❝ They never meet but there's a skirmish of wit between them *(I, i)*

He wears his faith but as the fashion of his hat *(I, i)*

Shall I never see a bachelor of threescore again? *(I, i)*

Thou wilt never get thee a husband, if thou be so shrewd of thy tongue *(II, i)*

As merry as the day is long *(II, i)*

Lord, I could not endure a husband with a beard on his face: I had rather lie in the woollen *(II, i)*

There was a star danced, and under that was I born *(II, i)*

Save in the office and affairs of love: / Therefore all hearts in love use their own tongues; / Let every eye negotiate for itself / And trust no agent *(II, i)*

Some Cupid kills with arrows, some with traps *(III, i)*

Every one can master a grief but he that has it *(II, ii)*

O villain! thou wilt be condemned into everlasting redemption for this *(IV, ii)* ❞

The Tragedy of King Richard II

King Richard summons two feuding nobles to his presence — Henry Bolingbroke is accusing Thomas Mowbray, Duke of Norfolk, of murdering the king's uncle, the Duke of Gloucester — Richard decrees they must decide the issue by combat — but just as they are about to duel, he halts proceedings and banishes them both — Bolingbroke's father, John of Gaunt, is ailing — the king visits him and there is acrimony between them — when Gaunt dies, Richard seizes his property to fund his coming expedition to Ireland— leaving his uncle, the Duke of York, as regent, the king sets off to campaign in Ireland —Bolingbroke returns to England, where Northumberland and other nobles swear loyalty to him — Bolingbroke claims his rightful inheritance from John of Gaunt and executes two of Richard's supporters, Bushy and Green — when Richard returns to Wales to meet the rebellion, Bolingbroke advances against him, his forces swelling and now joined by Richard's uncle, the Duke of York — at Flint Castle, Richard resigns himself to his fate — but when Bolingbroke attempts compromise, the king rejects his offers — Richard becomes Bolingbroke's prisoner — Bolingbroke attempts to find the truth about Gloucester's murder, and when Carlisle denounces him, Bolingbroke has him arrested — Richard abdicates and Bolingbroke becomes King Henry IV— on his way to the Tower of London, Richard tells his Queen, Isabel, to go to France — but now the Abbot of Westminster and York's son, Aumerle, conspire against the new king — York discovers this and hastens to warn Henry — Aumerle is spared upon his mother's appeal — a courtier, Sir Piers of Exton, overhears Henry rashly say, "Have I no friend will rid me of this living fear?" — he hastens to Pomfret, where the deposed king is deep in thought, comparing his cell to a world peopled with his thoughts — Exton enters Richard's cell and there is a fight — Richard is killed — Exton takes the body to Windsor Castle — and Henry IV, is consumed with remorse, vowing to go on a crusade to atone

DRAMATIS PERSONAE

King Richard II .... King of England
Queen Isabel...his wife
Edmund of Langley .... Duke of York, uncle to the King
Duchess of York..his wife
Duke of Aumerle... her son
John of Gaunt............... Duke of Lancaster, uncle to the King
Henry Bolingbroke........................... his son, Duke of Hertford
Thomas Mowbray.. Duke of Norfolk
Earl of Northumberland
Henry Percy ("Hotspur").. his son
Duchess of Gloucester.............. kinswoman to John of Gaunt
....and to York
Lord Salisbury
Bishop of Carlisle
Sir Stephen Scroop
Abbot of Westminster
Sir Piers of Exton
Duke of Surrey, Earl of Salisbury ... noblemen loyal to Richard
Lord Berkeley
Lords Ross, Fitzwater and Willoughby............... supporters of
....Bolingbroke
Bushy, Bagot, Green .... Richard's favourites

© THIRD MILLENNIUM PRESS LTD, 2005

> This royal throne of kings, this scepter'd isle, / This earth of majesty, this seat of Mars, / This other Eden, demi-paradise, / This fortress built by Nature for herself / Against infection and the hand of war, / This happy breed of men, this little world, / This precious stone set in the silver sea, / Which serves it in the office of a wall, / Or as a moat defensive to a house, / Against the envy of less happier lands, / This blessed plot, this earth, this realm, this England *(II, i)*
>
> The ripest fruit first falls *(II, i)*
>
> O! call back yesterday, bid time return. *(III, ii)*
>
> Let's talk of graves, of worms and epitaphs; / Make dust our paper, and with rainy eyes / Write sorrow on the bosom of the earth; / Let's choose executors and talk of wills *(III, ii)*
>
> For God's sake, let us sit upon the ground / And tell sad stories of the death of kings: / How some have been deposed, some slain in war, / Some haunted by the ghosts they have deposed; / some poisoned by their wives, some sleeping killed; / All murdered: for within the hollow crown / That rounds the mortal temples of a king / Keeps Death his court ... *(III, ii)*

Above: John of Gaunt bids farewell to his son, Bolingbroke, sent into exile by the king. "Come, come, my son. I'll bring thee on thy way. Had I thy youth and cause, I would not stay.
BOLINGBROKE: *"Then, England's ground, farewell; sweet soil, adieu: My mother, and my nurse, that bears me yet! Where'er I wander, boast of this I can, Though banish'd, yet a true-born Englishman." (I, iii)*

Above: Richard II (1189–99), a weak and vacillating king, who makes the fatal mistake of antagonising the nobility. Deposed, and in his cell at Pomfret, he muses in melancholy: "Thus play I in one person many people, And none contented; sometimes I am king; Then treasons make me wish myself a beggar, And so I am: then crushing penury Persuades me I was better when a king: Then am I king'd again; and by and by Think that I am unking'd by Bolingbroke, And straight am nothing: but whate'er I be, Nor I nor any man that but man is With nothing shall be pleas'd, till he be eas'd With being nothing." (V, v)

Written between 1595 and 1597, *Richard II* was first published in quarto format in 1597, and may have been performed before then. Exploring such themes as the divine right of kings, chivalry and loyalty, it is the prologue to Shakespeare's series on the Wars of the Roses.

Right: Richard, deposed and on his way to the Tower, bids adieu to Isabel. "Good sometime queen, prepare thee hence for France; Think I am dead, and that even here thou tak'st, As from my death-bed, thy last living leave. In winter's tedious nights sit by the fire With good old folks, and let them tell thee tales Of woeful ages, long ago betid; And ere thou bid good night, to quit their griefs, Tell thou the lamentable tale of me, And send the hearers weeping to their beds ..." (V, i)

King Henry IV

Part One — Henry IV prepares to go on crusade to atone for the murder of Richard II — meanwhile Glendower captures Mortimer, and Henry Hotspur defeats the Scots — meeting his victorious generals, the King contrasts the knightly Hotspur with his own son — for Prince Hal is leading a debauched life, with his friend, the fat old knight Falstaff — Worcester complains at his lack of reward for aiding Henry to attain the throne, and Hotspur wants to exchange his prisoners for Mortimer, his brother-in-law — thus he and Worcester fall out with the King — Hotspur joins Glendower, Douglas and the Archbishop of York in rebellion — Falstaff's band meanwhile rob pilgrims near Rochester but are relieved of their booty by the disguised Hal and friends — at the Boar's Head the joke is revealed — Falstaff hides and falls asleep — Hal pledges to make good the pilgrims' losses — Hotspur, Glendower and Mortimer plan their campaign — in London, Henry rebukes Hal for his debauchery, and the prince promises to reform — at the Boar's Head, he tells Falstaff he is to lead a band of men to battle — near Shrewsbury, Hotspur discovers that he must fight without Glendower and Northumberland — the King attempts to end the rebellion by negotiation, but fails — the battle is won by the royal army — Douglas kills Blunt — Hal is wounded but saves his father from Douglas and kills Hotspur in single combat — Hal seeks mercy for Douglas, but Westmoreland is condemned to death — and Henry prepares to fight Northumberland and Glendower — **Part Two** — Northumberland hears of the battle — the Lord Chief Justice upbraids Falstaff for his bad influence on Hal and sends him to campaign against the rebels — at York, Hastings, Mowbray and Bardolph plan — at the Boar's Head there is a brawl as sheriffs try to arrest Falstaff for non-payment of his bills — Falstaff dines with Mistress Quickly and Pistol tries to seduce Doll — Hal and Poins in disguise eavesdrop and hear ill of themselves — Falstaff is sent off to fight — he recruits in Gloucestershire — in Yorkshire, the rebels, Scroop, Hastings and Mowbray, are offered protection if they will disband — when they do, the royalist commanders Westmoreland and Lancaster renege and arrest them — Falstaff captures a prisoner without a fight — the King is saddened at Hal's continuing carousing with Falstaff and friends — Hal arrives as the ill Henry sleeps — thinking him dead, Hal is caught trying on the crown — but father and son are reconciled, and Henry advises Hal to pursue war abroad when he becomes king — Henry dies and Hal becomes King Henry V — Falstaff hurries to London, only to be publicly rejected by the new king and arrested

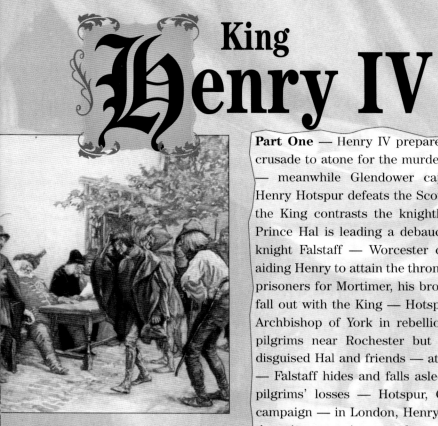

Above: Falstaff recruits. "Fie! This is hot weather, gentlemen. Have you provided me here half-a-dozen sufficient men?" (II, ii) Their names are Ralph Mouldy, Simon Shadow, Thomas Wart, Francis Feeble and Peter Bullcalf.

Henry IV, Part One, was written about 1596–7, performed in the latter year and first published in quarto in 1598. Acclaimed by many as Shakespeare's greatest history play, it is set in the years 1400–3 and is concerned with honour, courage and kingship, mixing history and comedy. The second play, *Henry IV, Part Two*, was written around 1597–8 and published in quarto 1600, having been performed several times by then. It covers the years 1403–14 and explores such themes as betrayal and justice.

© THIRD MILLENNIUM PRESS LTD, 2005

Above left: King Henry IV (1399–1413).

Above: Prince Hal undertakes to his father that he will henceforth conduct himself as more befits a prince, Henry having reminded him of the knightly Harry Percy. "The time will come, That I shall make this northern youth exchange His glorious deeds for my indignities. Percy is but my factor, good my lord, To engross up glorious deeds on my behalf; and I will call him to so strict account, That he shall render every glory up, Yea, even the slightest worship of his time, Or I will tear the reckoning from his heart. This in the name of God I promise here: The which if He be pleased I shall perform, I do beseech your majesty may salve The long-grown wounds of my intemperance: If not, the end of life cancels all bands; And I will die a hundred thousand deaths Ere break the smallest parcel of this vow." (1, III, ii)

> He will give the devil his due *(1, I, ii)*

I know a trick worth two of that *(1, II, i)*

It would be argument for a week, laughter for a month, and a good jest for ever *(1, II, ii)*

Out of this nettle, danger, we pluck this flower, safety *(1, II, iii)*

Is it not strange that desire should so many years outlive performance *(1, II, iv)*

Two stars keep not their motion in one sphere *(1, V, iv)*

The better part of valour is discretion *(1, V, iv)*

Away, you scullion! you rampallion! You fustilarian! I'll tickle your catastrophe *(2, II, i)*

He hath eaten me out of house and home *(2, II, i)*

Uneasy lies the head that wears the crown *(2, III, i)*

We have heard the chimes at midnight *(2, III, ii)*

A man can die but once; we owe God a death *(2, III, ii)*

Thy wish was father, Harry, to that thought *(2, IV, v)*

I know thee not, old man: fall to thy prayers / How ill white hairs become a fool and jester! *(2, V, v)* 〞

DRAMATIS PERSONAE

King Henry IV	King of England
Prince Hal (Harry)	Prince of Wales
John, Duke of Lancaster	
Humphrey, Duke of Gloucester	} his brothers
Thomas, Duke of Clarence	
Henry Percy	Earl of Northumberland
Hotspur (also Henry Percy)	his son
Sir John Falstaff	friend to Prince Hal
Earl of Westmoreland	
Sir Walter Blunt	
Thomas Percy	Earl of Worcester
Edmund Mortimer	Earl of March
Owen Glendower	leader of the Welsh rebels
Archibald	Earl of Douglas
Sir Richard Vernon	
Richard Scroop	
Mistress Quickly	hostess of the Boar's Head
Ned Poins, Peto, Bardolph, Gadshill	} drinkers at the Boar's Head
Earl of Warwick	
Earl of Surrey	
Earl of Westmoreland	a rebel leader
Gower, Harcourt, Sir John Blunt	
Ancient Pistol	a soldier
Archbishop of York	a rebel
Mowbray and Hastings	rebel leaders
Doll Tearsheet	Falstaff's favourite harlot

Left: Sir John Falstaff and Mistress Quickly, to whom he owes money. "A hundred mark is a long one for a poor lone woman to bear; and I have borne, and borne, and borne; and have been fubbed off, and fubbed off, and fubbed off, from this day to that day, it is a shame to be thought on. There is no honesty in such dealing; unless a woman should be made an ass, and a beast, to bear every knave's wrong.' (2, II, i) But as usual the fat knight manages to talk his way out.

Richard III

Written around 1592, *Richard III* was published in quarto in 1597, having received its first performance in 1593. Immensely popular in Shakespeare's lifetime, this is as much political propaganda in favour of the Tudors as it is drama. It completes Shakespeare's cycle of historical plays with one of the stage's greatest villains, ambitious, ruthless and shocking, a superb part for an actor to interpret.

Left: Richard III (1483–1485)

Richard, Duke of Gloucester, sets out on his plan to usurp the throne — he convinces King Edward of their brother Clarence's treason, for which he is sent to the Tower — at the funeral of Henry VI, Richard woos Anne, widow of Henry's son, whom Richard has killed — she is also daughter of another of his victims, Warwick — Richard accuses Queen Elizabeth of turning the king against Clarence, and Queen Margaret, widow of Henry VI, predicts Richard's true nature — in the Tower, Clarence has a nightmare, then Richard's henchmen arrive and stab him, then finish him off in a butt of malmsey wine — Richard still manages to make the king think their brother's death is his own fault, which adds to his infirmity — Edward dies, and Richard makes a show of consoling Queen Elizabeth — she now hears that Richard has arrested Lord Rivers, her brother, and Lord Grey, the son of her first marriage — afraid of Richard, she takes her youngest son, the Duke of York, to a place of sanctuary — meanwhile her elder son, Edward, Prince of Wales and now heir to the throne, is being brought to London by Buckingham for coronation — the Duke of York is seized and both boys are installed in the royal apartments at the Tower — Richard confides his plans to Buckingham, whose task it will be to convince everyone that the two young princes are illegitimate — as part of the charade, Buckingham publicly begs Richard to take the throne himself — Richard ostentatiously declines but then, with feigned reluctance, accepts — Elizabeth, Duchess of York, and Anne are refused access to the princes in the Tower, and Derby summons a shocked Anne to Westminster to be crowned queen — Richard III is crowned — but now he wants the princes murdered, and Buckingham hesitates — instead, the new king sends Sir James Tyrrel — meanwhile Catesby, at Richard's behest, spreads the rumour that Anne is dying for Richard plans to marry Edward IV's daughter, Elizabeth — Buckingham reminds Richard of his promise of an earldom, but Richard dismisses him, and Buckingham departs to join Richmond, Lancastrian pretender to the throne, in France — at the Tower, Tyrrel murders the little princes — when Queen Elizabeth and the Duchess of York tell Queen Margaret of the princes' deaths, she laments that her prophesies about Richard are coming true — when Richard tells Queen Elizabeth that he will marry her daughter she forbids it — but now the pretender to the throne is on the march — Richard mobilises Salisbury and Norfolk, but Derby hesitates, so Richard takes his son, George Stanley, hostage for Derby's cooperation — Buckingham is captured and executed, while Richmond lands, and the two armies converge upon Bosworth field — Richmond threatens Derby with his son's life, but Derby promises Richmond he will fight for him — that night, the ghosts of Richard's victims visit him in his sleep bringing messages of despair — they also visit his rival, Richmond, but bring encouragement — the battle is afoot, but Derby does not come to Richard's aid, and the king has Stanley executed — Norfolk too delays — the battle ends in defeat for Richard — unhorsed, he fights to the death — Derby finds the fallen crown and gives it to Richmond, who announces that he will marry Edward IV's daughter Elizabeth and thus unite the red and white roses — he will reign as Henry VII and bring the Wars of the Roses to an end

Above: Richard, Duke of Gloucester. "And therefore, since I cannot prove a lover, To entertain these fair well-spoken days, I am determined to prove a villain And hate the idle pleasures of these days." (I, i)

DRAMATIS PERSONAE

King Edward IV .... King of England
Queen Elizabeth ....his wife
Princes in the Tower .... sons of Edward IV
Elizabeth .... daughter of Queen Elizabeth
Richard, Duke of Gloucester ⎱ brothers to
George, Duke of Clarence ⎰ the king
Duchess of York.................. widowed mother of
....................................the king and his brothers
Queen Margaret.................... widow of Henry VI
Lady Anne... widow of Edward, son of Henry VI
Duke of Buckingham
Ratcliff, Catesby .... supporters of Richard
Dorset, Rivers, Grey........ kinsmen of Elizabeth
Richmond .... pretender to the throne,
.... and the future King Henry VII
Hastings
Derby

© THIRD MILLENNIUM PRESS LTD, 2005

> " Now is the winter of our discontent
> Made glorious summer by this sun of
> York *(I, i)*

I, that am curtail'd of this fair proportion, / Cheated of feature by dissembling nature, / Deform'd, unfinish'd, sent before my time / Into this breathing world, scare half made up, / And that so lamely and unfashionable / That dogs bark at me as I halt by them *(I, i)*

Why strew'st thou sugar on that bottled spider, / Whose deadly web ensnareth thee about? (I, iii)
So wise so young, they say, do never live long *(III, i)*

I am not in the giving vein to-day *(IV, ii)*

A horse! a horse! My kingdom for a horse! *(V, iv)* "

Above: On the night before Bosworth, the ghosts of Richard's victims visit him. Each identifies himself, ending, "To-morrow in the battle think on me, And fall thy edgeless sword: despair and die! (V, iii)

Left: Queen Elizabeth, the old Duchess of York, Anne, the Duchess of Gloucester, and Lady Margaret Plantagenet, young daughter of the murdered Clarence, stand outside the Tower, wherein the young princes are incarcerated. "Pity, you ancient stones, those tender babes Whom envy hath immured within your walls! Rough cradle for such little pretty ones!" (IV, i) They will never see the children again.

Henry VI

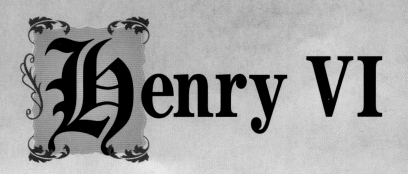

Henry VI
(1422–1461, 1470–1471)

Edward IV
(1461–1470, 1471–1483)

These three plays take up the story upon the death of Henry V and were written about 1590–1. *Part One* was published in the First Folio of 1623; *Part Two* in quarto in 1594; and *Part Three* in quarto the following year. They are concerned with feuding between English nobles, the continuing war in France, intrigues and changing alliances, and at centre, the succession to the throne. In *Part Three* begin the Wars of the Roses, the story of which concludes in *Richard III*.

DRAMATIS PERSONAE

King Henry VI .... King of England
Margaret of Anjou .... Queen to Henry VI
Edward, Prince of Wales .... their son
Duke of Gloucester........................... regent for the young king
Eleanor... his wife
Winchester / Beaufort .... churchman, enemy of Gloucester
Richard Plantagenet .... heir to the dukedom of York
Edward, later King Edward IV ⎫
Richard, later Duke of Gloucester ⎬ his sons
George, later Duke of Clarence ⎭
Rutland
Mortimer.. York's uncle
Talbot .... English comander-in-chief in France
Somerset .... a Lancastrian noble
Suffolk ⎫
Bedford ⎪
Warwick ⎬ English nobles
Buckingham ⎪
Salisbury ⎪
Clifford ⎭
Jack Cade................................. a false pretender to the throne
Charles .... Dauphin, later King of France
Louis IX .... King of France
Joan la Pucelle .... Joan of Arc, the "Maid of Orleans"
Lady Bona...................................... sister to the King of France
Lady Grey .... King Edward's bride

Part One — At the funeral of Henry V, the nobles discuss the bad state of affairs in France — Bedford goes to France as regent for the young King Henry VI, while Gloucester remains in England as Protector — Salisbury repels the newly crowned French King Charles from Orleans — but Joan la Pucelle convinces Charles she can defeat the English — Gloucester and Winchester are meanwhile feuding — Joan takes Orleans, and Salisbury is killed —but Talbot retakes Orleans — in the Temple Garden in London, leading nobles take sides, Yorkists plucking white roses as their emblem, Lancastrians red — the battle lines are being drawn for the Wars of the Roses — Richard Plantagenet visits his uncle, Mortimer, in the Tower of London — on his death-bed, Mortimer (erstwhile pretender to the crown) tells Richard that he must be the new claimant to the throne — Henry restores Richard's dukedom of York and plans to be crowned King of France in Paris — near Rouen, Joan persuades Burgundy to change sides — in Paris, Henry orders Talbot to attack Burgundy, directing Somerset and York to lay aside their differences and reinforce him — but when Charles attacks Talbot, York and Somerset fail to support him — Talbot and his son are killed — near Angiers, York captures Joan, while Suffolk captures Margaret, beautiful daughter of the Duke of Anjou — the English take Joan to be burnt at the stake — she curses the English — peace is agreed between Charles and Henry, the latter deciding to marry Margaret of Anjou — Suffolk plans to use her to control the king — **Part Two** — Suffolk brings Margaret to London to marry Henry, while England makes territorial concessions in France — Beaufort, Buckingham and Somerset conspire against Gloucester, and his wife is arrested for witchcraft — York explains his claim to the throne to Salisbury and Warwick, who espouse his cause — Gloucester's wife is paraded through the streets of London in rags before being banished — Gloucester is arrested for treason — the king sends York to Ireland to suppress a rebellion — while York encourages a rising by Jack Cade — Gloucester's murder is announced, and Warwick accuses Suffolk of the crime — Suffolk is banished — at sea, he is intercepted and killed — Cade's rebellion reaches London, but his supporters disperse and Cade is killed in flight — York returns from Ireland and marches on London, demanding Somerset's arrest as a traitor — Salisbury and Warwick support York — at the battle of St Albans, York's son, Richard, kills Somerset — **Part Three** — Henry and York agree that Henry will rule until he dies, then the succession will be with York's line — Queen Margaret angrily disagrees — at Sandal Castle, York's sons urge him to seize the throne at once — Margaret comes north with a large army — at the battle of Wakefield, York is captured and executed — York's eldest son Edward meets the Lancastrians in battle at Towton — Henry is discovered hiding in a forest, lamenting the horrors of civil war, and is arrested — while Warwick sets off for France to arrange the marriage of the new King Edward IV with the French king's kinswoman, Lady Bona, Edward makes his brother Richard Duke of York, and George Duke of Clarence — Margaret and the Prince of Wales beg help from King Louis IX of France, but he approves Warwick's planned marriage of Lady Bona to Edward — then comes news that Edward has married Lady Grey — Lewis is insulted — Warwick feels betrayed, changes sides and takes an army to England — Clarence also changes sides — Warwick captures Edward then heads for London, where Henry makes him his chief minister and Clarence Protector — at York, Gloucester rescues Edward — Edward seizes Henry — the armies maneouvre, and Warwick and Edward negotiate while Warwick waits for Clarence's reinforcements — but Clarence changes sides again — at the battle of Barnet, Warwick is killed — at the battle of Tewkesbury, Margaret is defeated and captured — her son is immediately dispatched — Gloucester hastens to London and confronts Henry in the Tower — the king, deposed again, predicts Gloucester's bloody future — and Gloucester stabs him to death — Edward resumes the throne, entreating love between his wife and his brothers

Above left: Joan la Pucelle in battle. Captured and led away to be burnt at the stake, she curses: "May never glorious sun reflect his beams Upon the country where you make abode: But darkness and gloomy shade of death Environ you, till mischief and despair Drive you to break your necks or hang yourselves!" (1, V, iv)

Left: The Temple Garden, London. SOMERSET: *"Hath not thy rose a thorn, Plantagenet?"* PLANTAGENET: *" Ay, sharp and piercing, to maintain his truth; Whiles thy consuming canker eats his falsehood."* SOMERSET: *"Well, I'll find friends to wear my bleeding roses, That shall maintain what I have said is true, Where false Plantagenet dare not be seen."* PLANTAGENET: *"Now by this maiden blossom in my hand, I scorn thee and thy faction, peevish boy ... Will I forever and my faction wear, until it wither with me to my grave Or flourish to the height of my degree." (1, II, iv)*

Above: After Towton, Henry wanders, lamenting his fate. " No, Harry, Harry, 'tis no throne of thine; Thy place is fill'd, thy sceptre wrung from thee, Thy balm wash'd off wherewith thou wast anointed: No bending knee will call thee Caesar now, No humble suitors press to speak for right, No, not a man comes for redress of thee: For how can I help them, and not myself?" (3, III, i)

> ❝ Smooth runs the water where the brook is deep *(2, III, i)*
>
> The first thing we do, let's kill all the lawyers *(2, IV, ii)*
>
> Patience is for poltroons *(3, I, i)*
>
> The smallest worm will turn being trodden on *(3, II, ii)*
>
> Down, down to hell; and say I sent thee thither *(3, V, vi)*
>
> The midwife wonder'd, and the women cried 'O! Jesus bless us, he is born with teeth!' And so I was; which plainly signified That I should snarl and bite and play the dog *(3, V, vi)* ❞

King Henry V

Henry V, 1413–1422

Charles VI of France

Above: Archers in combat. The longbow is Henry's key weapon at the battle of Agincourt.

> O! for a Muse of fire, that would ascend
> The brightest heaven of invention
> *(Chorus)*
>
> This day is called the feast of Crispian:
> He that outlives this day and comes safe
> home, / Will stand a tip-toe when this day is
> named, / And rouse him at the name of
> Crispian *(IV, iii)*
>
> Old men forget: yet all shall be forgot, / But
> he'll remember with advantages / What feats
> he did that day. Then shall our names, /
> Familiar in his mouth as household words /
> Harry the King, Bedford and Exeter, /
> Warwick and Talbot, Salisbury and
> Gloucester, / Be in their flowing cups freshly
> remembered *(IV, iii)*
>
> We few, we happy few, we band of brothers: /
> For he today that sheds his blood with me /
> Shall be my brother; be he ne'er so vile / This
> day shall gentle his condition / And
> gentlemen in England now a-bed / Shall think
> themselves accursed they were not here, /
> And hold their manhoods cheap whiles any
> speaks / That fought with us upon
> Saint Crispin's day. *(IV, iii)*

Prince Hal's transformation from dissipated youth to responsible monarch is marvelled upon by the Archbishop of Canterbury and the Bishop of Ely — they discuss the French law of royal succession and urge Henry to pursue his claim to the French throne — the Dauphin's ambassador tells Henry there is naught for him in France and brings a gift of tennis balls — angered, Henry warns him that this insult "hath turned his balls into gunstones" — the French hire three English nobles, the Earl of Cambridge, Lord Scroop and Sir Thomas Grey, to assassinate Henry, but the plot is discovered — at the Boar's Head, Henry's old drinking companions discuss marital arrangements and then hear that Falstaff is seriously ill — at Southampton, the King has the three conspirators executed — Pistol announces that Falstaff is dead, and his old friends hasten to join the expedition to France — the army crosses the Channel — at the palace of the French king, the Dauphin scorns the invasion, but Charles VI and the Constable of France warn him that Henry is a changed man — Exeter arrives with the message that the French king must surrender to Henry's demands and that the Dauphin can expect punishment for the tennis-ball insult — the English besiege Harfleur — Charles offers Henry the hand of his daughter, Katherine, in marriage, together with "some petty ... dukedoms", but to no avail — Henry orders the attack on Harfleur, in which the Boar's Head band participate after some hesitation — the French envoy, Montjoy, invites Henry to depart — but now a major battle looms — the night before, Henry disguises himself as a Welshman, Harry Le Roy, and mingles with the troops to discover their mood — the battle of Agincourt ensues, and Henry makes a rousing speech before the fight begins — the battle won, the victors make a jubilant return to England — several years pass — then Henry leads another expedition to France — in camp, Pistol and Fluellen fall out over a leek, then mourn the death of Nell Quickly — Henry meets the French king and sets out his terms for peace — Henry woos the king's daughter — then the French accept his terms — Henry is to inherit the throne of France and takes Katherine as his bride — an epilogue looks forward to the dismal career of the outcome of this marriage, King Henry VI

Above: Despite the language barrier, Henry woos Princess Katherine of France. "I' faith, Kate, my wooing is fit for thy understanding: I am glad thou canst speak no better English; for if thou couldst, thou wouldst find me such a plain king that thou would'st think I had sold my farm to buy my crown. I know no ways to mince it in love, but directly to say 'I love you'; then if you urge me further than to say 'Do you in faith?' I wear out my suit. Give me your answer; i' faith do: and so clap hands and a bargain. How say you, lady?" KATHERINE: "Sauf votre honneur, me understand vell." (V, ii)

Written about 1598–9 and published in quarto in 1600, *Henry V* is one of the most popular of Shakespeare's history plays, a tale of courage and patriotism, with rousing speeches, but also continuing the story of Henry's old friends

Below: Henry at Agincourt. At one point the French kill the English page boys, contrary to the laws of war. "I was not angry since I came to France Until this instant. Take a trumpet, herald; Ride thou unto the horsemen on yon hill: If they will fight with us, bid them come down, Or void the field; they do offend our sight. If they do neither, we will come to them ... And not a man of them shall we take Shall taste our mercy." (IV, vii)

DRAMATIS PERSONAE

King Henry V	recently crowned King of England
Dukes of Clarence, Bedford, Gloucester	his brothers
Dukes of Westmoreland, Salisbury, Warwick	Henry's advisers
Duke of Exeter	uncle or cousin to the king
Archbishop of Canterbury	
Bishop of Ely	
Cambridge, Scoop, Grey	conspirators
Duke of York	cousin to the king
Duke of Suffolk	
Fluellen, Macmorris, Jamy, Capt Gower	English captains
Charles VI	King of France
Queen Isabel	his wife
Katherine	their daughter
The Dauphin	son to the King of France
Constable of France	
Duke of Orleans	
Duke of Bourbon	
Earl of Granpré	
Lord Rambures	
Duke of Burgundy	
Governor of Harfleur	
Sir Thomas Erpingham	
Mistress Quickly	Hostess of the Boar's Head tavern
Montjoy	French herald